The Last Day

The Last Day

Readers Script
A Readers Theater Presentation

Richard P. Zimmerman

NOVO CIVITAS BOOKS AND RESOURCES, SEATTLE, WASHINGTON

The Last Day
Readers Script

A Readers Theater Presentation

Richard P. Zimmerman

© 2021 Richard P. Zimmerman

All rights reserved. No part of this book may be reproduced by any means without written permission of the publisher except for brief quotations in reviews.

Permission is granted to the owner of this book to present live performances of this play. No electronic recording, transmission, or broadcast of this book is permitted in any way.

Scripture quotations are an original translation by the author.

Novo Civitas Books and Resources

www.novocivitas.com

ISBN 9780578337470

Jesus knew that the time had come for him to leave this world and go to the Father. Having loved his own who were in the world, he now showed them the full measure of his love.

John 13:1

Contents

Character List
Act I   1
Act II   33

The Last Day

———————

A Play In 2 Acts

by Richard P. Zimmerman

Character List
In order of appearance

Voices – ACT I
    Narrator 1
    Jesus
    Narrator 2
    Peter
    John
    Disciples
    One Disciple
    Thomas
    Philip
    Judas (not Iscariot)
    Judas Iscariot
    Crowd of Soldiers

VOICES – ACT II
    Narrator 1
    Narrator 2
    Servant Woman 1
    Peter
    Jesus
    Attendant of the High Priest

Servant Woman 2
Man Standing By The Fire
Servant of the High Priest (standing by the fire)
False Witness
Caiaphas
Crowd of Priests
Judas Iscariot
One of the Chief Priests
Pilate
Pilate's Wife
Crowd
Soldiers
Priests and Attendants
Soldier
First Criminal
Second Criminal
First Passerby
Scribe
Second Passerby
Centurion (Soldier)
A Detachment of Soldiers

ACT ONE

Introduction and Welcome
This is an opportunity for helping guests to feel at ease and to set the tone for worship. It may be best for a pastor or other leader to take this part.

Opening Prayer

> Prelude

A brief instrumental musical piece could be played here to set the tone.

SETTING: Somewhere outside the city of Jerusalem; possibly across the Kidron Valley in Bethany.

> NARRATOR 1
> When the day of unleavened bread came, the day on which the Passover lamb had to be sacrificed, Jesus sent two of his disciples, Peter and John, and he told them,

> JESUS
> Go prepare a place for us to eat the Passover.

The Last Day

NARRATOR 2
They asked,

PETER AND JOHN
Where should we prepare it?

NARRATOR 1
He answered,

JESUS
When you enter the city gate you will see a man carrying a pitcher of water; follow him and where he enters a house you will follow him in. Tell the owner of the house, "The Teacher says, 'My time is near. I am going to observe the Passover with my disciples at your house. Where is the guest room where I am to eat the Passover with my disciples?'

He will show you a spacious room on an upper floor, furnished. Prepare for us there.

NARRATOR 2
They went and found everything as he said, so they got everything ready for the Passover.

ACT ONE

Congregational Singing

(Suggested)

Twilight

In the first month, on the fourteenth day of the month, at twilight, is the Passover to the LORD.

Leviticus 23:5

At The Table

SETTING: An upstairs room in a residence in Jerusalem.

NARRATOR 1

When evening came Jesus was reclining at the table with the Twelve. It was just before the Passover Feast. Jesus knew that the time had come for him to leave this world and go to the Father. Having loved his own who were in the world, he now showed them the full measure of his love.

The Last Day

NARRATOR 2

The meal was being served, and the devil had already put into the heart Judas Iscariot, son of Simon, to betray Jesus. Knowing that the Father had given everything into his hands, and that he had been sent by God and was returning to God, Jesus got up from the meal, took off his outer clothes, took a towel, and wrapped it around his waist. Then he poured water into a basin. He began to wash his disciples' feet, and he dried them with the towel he had wrapped around himself.

NARRATOR 1

Then he came toward Simon Peter.

PETER

Lord, are you going to wash my feet?

JESUS

You do not understand now what I am doing, but you will understand later.

ACT ONE

PETER
Certainly not! You will never wash my feet.

JESUS
If I don't wash your feet you have no part in me.

PETER
Then, Lord, not only my feet but also my hands and my head!

JESUS
A person who has had a bath needs only to wash the feet; the rest of the body is clean. And you are clean, though not all of you.

NARRATOR 2
Jesus said this because he knew who would betray him, and that was why he said *you are not all clean.*

And so when he had finished washing feet he put his outer clothes back on and reclined again in his place.

The Last Day

JESUS
Can you comprehend what I have just done for you? You call me 'Teacher' and 'Lord,' which is right, because that is who I am. Since I, your Lord and Teacher, have washed your feet, you should also wash each other's feet. I have set an example for you to do for one another what I have done for you. I am telling you the truth; no servant is greater than his master. No messenger is greater than the one who sent the message. Now that you have learned this, you will be blessed if you do it.

Bread and Cup

NARRATOR 1
Then Jesus said to them,

JESUS
I have deeply desired to eat this Passover with you before I suffer. For I tell you, I will not eat it again until it finds fulfillment in the kingdom of God.

ACT ONE

NARRATOR 2
While they were eating, Jesus took bread, gave thanks and broke it, gave it to his disciples, and said,

JESUS
Take and eat; this is my body broken for you. Do this in remembrance of me.

NARRATOR 1
Then he took the cup, gave thanks and offered it to them, saying,

JESUS
Drink from it, all of you. This is my blood of the new covenant, which is poured out for many for the forgiveness of sins. Do this, whenever you drink it, as a way of remembering me.

AT THIS POINT IT WOULD BE APPROPRIATE TO PAUSE THE READING AND CELEBRATE THE LORD'S SUPPER IN WHATEVER WAY IS CUSTOMARY IN YOUR CONGREGATION.

Congregational Singing
(Suggested)

The Last Day

*Jesus Predicts
The Betrayal*

NARRATOR 2
Jesus was deeply troubled in spirit and he solemnly declared,

JESUS
I tell you truly, one of you is going to betray me.

NARRATOR 1
His disciples looked around at each another, completely uncertain as to which of them he meant. They were very sad and began to say to him one after another,

DISCIPLES
Not necessarily speaking together. The readers should speak the line in their own way. They will all speak at roughly the same time, but the tone and inflection will distinguish the voices among the chaos of them all speaking at once.

Surely not I, Lord?

NARRATOR 2
One disciple, one whom Jesus loved, was reclining next to him. Simon Peter motioned to that disciple and said,

ACT ONE

PETER
Ask him who he means.

NARRATOR 1
So the disciple leaned back toward Jesus and asked,

JOHN
Lord, who?

JESUS
The one who has dipped his hand into the bowl with me will betray me. The Son of Man will die just as it is written. But such misery will fall upon that man who betrays the Son of Man! It would be better if he had never been born. I will dip bread in a bowl and give it to the one who will betray me.

NARRATOR 2
Then he dipped the bread and gave it to Judas Iscariot, son of Simon. As soon as Judas took the bread, Satan entered into him.

JESUS
Hurry and do what you are about to do.

The Last Day

NARRATOR 1
But no one else at the table understood why Jesus said this. Since Judas was in charge of the money, some thought Jesus was telling him to buy things necessary for the Festival, or to give a gift to the poor. As soon as Judas received the bread he went out into the night.

A Dispute About Who Is Greatest

NARRATOR 2
An argument began among them about which of them ought to be regarded as the greatest. Jesus said to them,

ACT ONE

JESUS

Kings lord it over their nations and those who exert authority over others call themselves 'doers of good.' But that is not how it is with you. Instead, the greatest among you will be like the youngest, and the one who leads as the one who serves. For who is ordinarily considered greater, the one who sits at the table or the one who serves? Is it not the one who sits at the table? But I am with you as one who serves. Through all my trials you are the ones who have stood by me. Just as my Father gave me rightful reign I also confer on you a kingdom. You will eat and drink at my table in my kingdom and sit on thrones, ruling the twelve tribes of Israel.

The Last Day

*Jesus Predicts
Simon Peter
Will Deny
Him*

NARRATOR 1
With Judas gone, Jesus said,

JESUS
Children, I am with you for only a little while longer. You cannot follow me to where I am now going.

So I give you a new command: Love one another. As I have loved you, you must love one another. Everyone will know that you are my disciples because you love one another.

NARRATOR 2
Simon Peter asked,

PETER
Lord, where are you going?

JESUS
You cannot follow where I am going now, but you will follow me later.

(Continued)

ACT ONE

JESUS *(continuing)*

Simon, Simon, pay attention! Satan has requested to sift you as wheat. But I have prayed that your faith may not fail you, Simon. And when you return, strengthen your brothers.

PETER

Lord, why can't I follow you now? I am prepared to go to prison with you and even to die. Even if everyone scatters because of you, I never will.

JESUS

Peter, will you really lay down your life for me? I must tell you, before the rooster crows twice today, you will deny you know me three times.

PETER
repeating insistently

Even if I die with you, I will never deny you.

NARRATOR 1

All the other disciples also said the same thing.

The Last Day

*What Is
Needed For
This New
Mission*

NARRATOR 1
Then Jesus asked,

JESUS
When I sent you out without a wallet, a bag or sandals, did you lack anything?

DISCIPLES
Nothing.

JESUS
But now if you have money, take it, and also a bag. And if you don't have a sword, sell your cloak and buy one. As it is written in the scriptures: 'And he was counted among the rebels;' I tell you this will come true in me. Yes, what is written about me is coming to fulfillment.

NARRATOR 2
The disciples said,

ACT ONE

ONE DISCIPLE (FOR ALL)
Here, Lord, look. We have two swords.

JESUS
That is enough.

Jesus Teaches
The Disciples
At The Table

JESUS
Do not let your hearts be anxious. Trust in God and trust in me. There are many rooms in my Father's house. If it were not so, I would never have told you that I am going to prepare a place for you. Since I am going to prepare a place for you, I will come back and take you to be with me so that we can be together. You know where I am going and you know the way.

NARRATOR 2
Thomas said,

The Last Day

THOMAS
We don't know where you are going, Lord, so how could we know the way?

JESUS
I am the way and the truth and the life. No one comes to the Father except through me. If you knew me, you would also know my Father. From now on, you know him and have seen him.

NARRATOR 1
Philip said to him,

PHILIP
Lord, show us the Father and that will satisfy us.

JESUS
Even after I have been with you such a long time, Philip, don't you know me? The one who has seen me has seen the Father. How is it that you say, "Show us the Father?" Don't you believe that I am in the Father, and the Father is in me? The words I say to you are not just my own. But the Father, living in me, is doing his work.

ACT ONE

JESUS *(continuing)*

I tell you the truth, anyone who has faith in me will do what I have been doing, and will do even greater things than these, because I go to the Father. And whatever you ask in my name I will do, so that the Son will bring glory to the Father. If you ask for anything in my name I will do it.

If you love me, you will obey what I command. And I will ask the Father, and he will give you another Counselor to be with you in all times and ages—the Spirit of truth. This world is unable to receive him, because it neither sees him nor knows him. You know him because he stays with you and will be in you. I will not leave you abandoned. I will come to you. Soon the world will no longer see me, but you will see me. Because I live you will also live.

NARRATOR 2

Then Judas (now this was not Judas Iscariot) said,

The Last Day

JUDAS (NOT ISCARIOT)
Why do you intend to reveal yourself to us, Lord, and not to the world?

JESUS
Those who love me will obey my words and my Father will love them. We will come to them and make our home with them. Anyone who does not love me will not regard my words. And these words you hear are not my own but my Father's who sent me.

This all I have told you while still with you. But the Father will send the Counselor in my name, the Holy Spirit, who will teach you everything and will cause you to remember all the things I have said to you. I leave peace with you. I give my peace to you. But I do not give as the world gives. So do not let your hearts be anxious and do not be fearful.

ACT ONE

*Departing From
The Upper Room*

NARRATOR 1
Jesus then said,

JESUS
Get up. We're going away from this place now.

NARRATOR 2
When they had sung a hymn, Jesus went out as usual to the Mount of Olives, and his disciples came with him.

The Last Day

SETTING: Walking from the residence in which the upstairs room was located to the garden of Gethsemane. The Temple would have been prominently visible during part of their walk. The Temple was well lit.

A prominent feature of the Temple decoration was a vine with clusters of grapes.

*Teaching Along
The Way From
The Upper
Room To The
Wadi Kidron*

JESUS
I am the true vine, and my Father is the vine-keeper. All of the branches in me that bear no fruit he cuts off, and he prunes every branch that does bear fruit so that it will bear even more fruit. You have been pruned by the things I have told you. Abide in me, and I will remain in you.

(Continued)

ACT ONE

JESUS *(continuing)*

Just as no branch can produce fruit by itself but it must remain in the vine, in that same way you cannot produce fruit unless you remain in me.

I am the vine, you are the branches. Those who remain in me and I in them will produce large crops of fruit. You can do nothing apart from me. The one who does not remain in me is like a cast off branch that withers. Workers pick up those branches, throw them into the fire and they are burned. If you abide in me and my words remain in you, ask whatever you will, and it will be created for you. My Father's glory is evident as you produce a large crop of fruit, and you grow more and more into becoming my disciples.

I have loved you as the Father has loved me. Remain in my love. As you obey my commands you remain in my love, just as I obey my Father's commands and remain in his love.

(Continued)

The Last Day

JESUS *(continuing)*
This I have told you in order that my joy may remain in you and that your joy may be completely full. My command is that you love one another as I have loved you. No one can have or demonstrate greater love than if you lay down your life for your friends. You are my friends if you do what I command. I don't call you servants any longer, because a servant does not know what the master is doing. Instead, I call you friends, because I have revealed everything to you that I learned from my Father. You did not choose me, but I chose you and appointed you to go and produce a crop of fruit that will last. So the Father will give you whatever you ask in my name. Here is my command: Love each other.

I have told you all of this, so that in me you may have peace. You will have affliction in this world. But be hopeful. I have conquered the world.

ACT ONE

NARRATOR 1
And having made this declaration Jesus lifted his vision toward heaven and said,

JESUS
Father, the hour is here. Glorify your Son, in order that your Son may glorify you, since you gave him rightful authority over all humanity so that he might give eternal life to all those you have given him. This, then, is eternal life: to know you, the one true God, and to know Jesus Christ, the one you sent. I glorified you on earth. I completed the work you gave me to do. So now glorify me together with you, Father, with the glory I had with you before the world was created.

The Last Day

*Crossing The
Kidron Valley
And Entering
The Garden*

SETTING: The Garden of Gethsemane

NARRATOR 2

Jesus now crossed the Wadi Kidron and his disciples went with him. On the other side there was a garden called Gethsemane on the Mount of Olives, and he and his disciples went into it.

JESUS

Sit here and pray that you won't come under temptation while I go over there and pray.

NARRATOR 1

He took Peter and the two sons of Zebedee, James and John, along with him, and he began to grieve and to be deeply distressed.

JESUS

My soul is overwhelmed with sorrow to the point of death. Stay here and keep watch with me.

ACT ONE

NARRATOR 2

Going about a stone's throw away, he fell with his face to the ground and asked that, if possible, this hour might pass him by.

JESUS

Abba, Father, you can do everything. May this cup be taken from me. Yet not as I want, but as you will.

NARRATOR 1

An angel from heaven then appeared to him, strengthening him. He continued praying even more earnestly. And drops of his sweat fell to the ground like drops of blood.

He got up from prayer, returned to his disciples and found them sleeping, exhausted by their grief.

JESUS

Why are you sleeping? Could all of you not keep watch with me for one hour?

Get up! Watch, and pray so that you won't come under temptation. The spirit is certainly willing but the body is weak.

The Last Day

NARRATOR 2

Going away a second time he again prayed,

JESUS

My Father, if this cup cannot be taken away unless I drink it, let your will be done.

NARRATOR 1

Again he found them sleeping when he returned because their eyes were heavy. So leaving them, he went away once more and prayed a third time, the same as before.

He then came to the disciples and said to them,

JESUS

Sleep now and rest. The hour is now arriving for the Son of Man to be betrayed into the hands of sinners. Look! Get up. Let's go! Here comes my betrayer!

ACT ONE

*The Arrest In
The Garden*

NARRATOR 2
Now the one betraying him, that is Judas, also knew this place, because Jesus often gathered with his disciples there. So Judas approached leading a band of soldiers and some officials from the chief priests and the Pharisees with lamps, lanterns, and armed with swords and clubs.

The one betraying him had set up a signal:

JUDAS ISCARIOT
Whoever I kiss is the one; apprehend him and take him away securely.

NARRATOR 1
Right away he came up to Jesus,

JUDAS ISCARIOT
Rabbi!

The Last Day

JESUS
Judas, would you use a kiss to betray the Son of Man?

NARRATOR 2
Knowing all that was going to happen to him, Jesus asked them,

JESUS
Who do you want?

CROWD OF SOLDIERS
Jesus the Nazarene.

NARRATOR 1
Jesus said to them,

JESUS
I am.

NARRATOR 2
Now Judas the betrayer stood right there with them. When Jesus said, "I am," they pulled back and fell on the ground.

He asked them again,

JESUS
Who do you want?

ACT ONE

CROWD OF SOLDIERS
Jesus the Nazarene.

JESUS
I said to you, 'I am.' So since you are looking for me, allow these others to go.

NARRATOR 1
These words he had spoken were fulfilled in this: "I lost none of those you gave me."

The men laid hands on Jesus and seized him.

Simon Peter had a sword. He drew it and struck the slave of the high priest, and cut off his right ear. The name of the slave was Malchus.

Jesus told Peter,

The Last Day

JESUS

Put your sword into its sheath! Father has given me this cup. Shall I not drink it? All who draw a sword will die by a sword. Or do you think I don't have the power to ask my Father to provide me at once with more than twelve legions of angels? But then how would the Scriptures be fulfilled that say it must be this way?

NARRATOR 2

And touching the ear, he cured him. Then the detachment of soldiers with its commander and the Jewish officials bound Jesus.

And Jesus said,

JESUS

As if I am a robber you have come out with swords and clubs to arrest me? I was with you daily in the temple courts teaching, and you did not arrest me. But this is how the Scriptures are fulfilled. This is your hour and the authority of darkness.

ACT ONE

NARRATOR 1

Then everyone left him and ran away. Now there was this young man following Jesus, and he was wearing nothing but a linen garment. And they took hold of him, but he left his garment behind and ran away naked.

END OF ACT 1

Congregational Singing Before Going Out (suggested) IF *the performance is to be held on two consecutive nights.*

ACT TWO

If the story is being presented in its entirety on one night then there is no need for a pause between Act I and Act II. But if the Two Acts are presented on consecutive evenings, then an opening introduction and brief recap will be a good idea. See the Song Suggestion Chart (PART ONE, Director's Notes, Chapter 8) for suggestions of music in this place if the presentation is to take place on consecutive nights.

Also, if the presentation is on two separate nights a brief welcome and opening prayer would be a good start to the evening's presentation.

NARRATOR 1

RECAP

(Only needed for a two-night presentation)

Jesus and his disciples had shared their last Passover meal together. Judas left the table and went out into the night to lead the guards to the garden, for he knew it was the custom of Jesus to go the garden of Gethsemane for prayer following the Passover meal. A contingent of guards came with Judas and arrested Jesus. The rest of the disciples scattered into the night while Jesus was taken for trial.

THE LAST DAY

*Jesus is Made
To Appear
Before the
Temple Leaders*

SETTING: The house of Annas,
Father–in–law of Caiaphas

NARRATOR 2
First they brought Jesus to Annas, the father-in-law of Caiaphas, who was the high priest that year. Caiaphas was the one who had advised the Jews that it would be desirable that one man would die for the people.

ACT TWO

*Peter Was
Following*

SETTING: A courtyard outside
the house of the high priest

NARRATOR 1

Now Simon Peter was following Jesus at a distance, along with another disciple. This disciple was known to the high priest, so he entered with Jesus into the high priest's courtyard, while Peter stood outside at the door. So the other disciple, the one known to the high priest, came back, spoke to the servant woman who was on duty at the door, and brought Peter in.

*Peter Denies
Knowing Jesus*

NARRATOR 2

It was cold, and the servants and officials stood around a fire they had kindled to keep warm. Peter also was standing with them, warming himself. When the servant woman saw Peter warming himself, she looked closely at him.

THE LAST DAY

SERVANT WOMAN 1
You aren't one of the disciples of that Nazarene, Jesus, are you?

PETER
I don't know him, woman.

Jesus Is Questioned by Annas

SETTING: The house of Annas, Father-in-law of Caiaphas

NARRATOR 1
Meanwhile, the high priest was questioning Jesus about his disciples and his teaching.

JESUS
I have spoken plainly to the world. I always taught in synagogues and in the temple, where all the Jews come together. I spoke nothing in secret. So why question me? Ask the people who heard me. They know what I said.

NARRATOR 2
When Jesus had said this, one of the attendants standing nearby slapped Jesus.

ACT TWO

ATTENDANT OF THE HIGH PRIEST
(in anger)
Is this how you answer the high priest?

JESUS
If I said something bad, explain to everyone what is wrong. But if I said something good, then why did you hit me?

NARRATOR 1
Annas then sent him to Caiaphas the high priest, still bound.

Peter Denies
Knowing Jesus
A Second Time

SETTING: A courtyard outside the house of the high priest

NARRATOR 2
Simon Peter was still standing by the fire warming himself. When the servant woman saw him there, she said again to those standing around,

The Last Day

SERVANT WOMAN 2
This is one of them.

MAN STANDING BY THE FIRE
You are with Jesus the Galilean too, aren't you?

PETER
I am not.

Peter Denies
Knowing Jesus
A Third Time

NARRATOR 1
But one of the servants of the high priest, a relative of the man whose ear Peter had cut off, said,

SERVANT OF THE HIGH PRIEST
Didn't I see you in the garden with him?

PETER
I swear, I don't know who you're talking about,

ACT TWO

NARRATOR 2
... and he went out into the entryway.

At that moment a rooster began to crow.

Immediately the rooster crowed a second time. Then Peter remembered what Jesus had told him:

JESUS
Before the rooster crows twice you will deny you know me three times.

NARRATOR 1
Then he was overcome with bitter weeping.

THE LAST DAY

*Jesus Is Tried
Before Caiaphas
and the Other
Leaders*

SETTING: A larger place for a trial before Caiaphas

NARRATOR 2

At dawn those who had arrested Jesus took him before Caiaphas high priest, and all the chief priests, the elders and the teachers of the law had assembled.

NARRATOR 1

Now the chief priests and the whole Sanhedrin were looking for false evidence against Jesus so that they could put him to death. But they did not find any. Though many false witnesses came forward, their statements did not agree. Eventually two came forward and said,

ACT TWO

FALSE WITNESS
We heard him say, 'I am able to destroy the temple of God made with human hands and build a temple not made with hands over the course of three days.'

NARRATOR 2
Yet even then their stories did not match one another.

Then the high priest arose and said to Jesus,

CAIAPHAS
Don't you have an answer to the accusations that these men are bringing against you?

NARRATOR 1
But Jesus stayed silent and gave no answer.

CAIAPHAS
I place you under oath by the living God. Tell us. Are you the Messiah, the Son of the Blessed One?

The Last Day

JESUS

I am. If I tell you, you do not believe me, and if I were to ask you a question, you would never answer. But I declare to all of you, from now on you will see the Son of Man sitting at the right hand of the Mighty One and coming on the clouds of heaven.

NARRATOR 2

Then the high priest tore his clothes.

CAIAPHAS

Now you have heard blasphemy! What is your decision?

CROWD OF PRIESTS

He deserves death!

NARRATOR 1

Then those who were holding him spit in his face. They blindfolded him and struck him with their fists.

ATTENDANT OF THE HIGH PRIEST

Prophesy for us, Christ! Who is it that hit you?

ACT TWO

NARRATOR 2
And the guards took him and beat him. And they hurled many other insults at him.

Jesus Is Turned Over To Pilate

SETTING: The *Praetorium*, the residential palace of the Roman governor, Pontius Pilate

NARRATOR 1
Then all of the chief priests and the elders of the people bound Jesus and they took him from Caiaphas to the *Praetorium*, the palace of the Roman governor. It was early morning, and to avoid ritual uncleanness they did not enter the *Praetorium*, because they wanted to be able to eat the Passover meal.

The Last Day

Judas Responds

SETTING: The Temple

NARRATOR 2

When Judas, who had betrayed him, saw that Jesus was condemned, he was filled with regret and took back the thirty pieces of silver to the chief priests and the elders.

JUDAS ISCARIOT

I have sinned. I betrayed an innocent man.

ONE OF THE CHIEF PRIESTS
(with disdain)

What is that to us? You see to it.

NARRATOR 1

So, throwing down the silver pieces in the temple, Judas left. And he went away and hanged himself.

NARRATOR 2

The chief priests picked up the silver pieces.

ACT TWO

ONE OF THE CHIEF PRIESTS
It is not in accordance with law to put these into the treasury, since it is the price of blood.

NARRATOR 1
They deliberated and agreed to use the money to buy the potter's field as a cemetery for foreigners. So because of this it has been called the Field of Blood to this day. Then what was spoken by Jeremiah the prophet was fulfilled: "They took the thirty silver pieces, his valuation set by the people of Israel, and they used them to buy the potter's field, as the Lord commanded me."

Trial Before Pilate

Pilate Asks What Charges Are Laid Against Jesus

SETTING: The *Praetorium*; the residential palace of the Roman governor, Pontius Pilate

NARRATOR 2
Pilate came outside to the whole gathering.

The Last Day

PILATE
What accusations are you bringing against this man?

ONE OF THE PRIESTS
We discovered this man corrupting our people. He forbids payment of taxes to Caesar and says he is Christ, a king. If he were not doing bad things, we would not have brought him to you.

PILATE
Take him yourselves and judge him according to your own law.

ONE OF THE CHIEF PRIESTS
But we are not authorized to kill anyone.

NARRATOR 1
This answer was to fulfill what Jesus had spoken about the kind of death he would die.

Pilate Asks Jesus, "Are You A King?"

So Pilate went back inside the *Praetorium*, summoned Jesus and said,

ACT TWO

PILATE
Are you the king of the Judeans?

JESUS
You have said so.

NARRATOR 2
But to the accusations by the chief priests and the elders, he gave no response.

PILATE
Don't you hear the many witnesses against you? Aren't you going to answer? Listen to how many accusations there are!

NARRATOR 1
But Jesus said nothing in response, and Pilate was astonished.

Pilate Sends Jesus To Herod

NARRATOR 2
Pilate again went out to the Judeans and announced to the chief priests and the crowd,

PILATE
I can't find a single charge against this man.

The Last Day

NARRATOR 1
But they were insistent.

ONE OF THE CHIEF PRIESTS
He incites people all over Judea with his teaching. He began in Galilee and has now come here.

NARRATOR 2
Pilate heard this and inquired if the man was a Galilean. So when he learned that Jesus belonged to Herod's jurisdiction, he transferred him to Herod, who was also in Jerusalem during those days.

Herod Questions Jesus

SETTING: The Palace of King Herod

NARRATOR 1
So Herod was very happy when he saw Jesus. He had wanted to see Jesus for a long time because, from what he had heard, he hoped to see a miraculous sign of some sort take place. He questioned him about many things, but Jesus gave no answer. The chief priests and the teachers of the law were standing nearby accusing him loudly.

ACT TWO

NARRATOR 2
Herod and his soldiers then treated him with scorn and mocked him. They dressed him in a magnificent robe and returned him to Pilate. Herod and Pilate became friends that day. They had been enemies before this.

Pilate Questions Jesus Again

SETTING: The *Praetorium*; the residential palace of the Roman governor, Pontius Pilate

NARRATOR 1
Pilate then went back inside the *Praetorium*, called Jesus and asked him,

PILATE
Are you the king of the Judeans?

JESUS
Do you say that of yourself, or did others say this to you about me?

PILATE
Am I Judean? These are your own people. The chief priests delivered you to me. What have you done?

The Last Day

JESUS
My kingdom is not of this world. If my reign were of this world my supporters would fight that I might not to be handed over by the Judeans. But my kingdom is not from this place.

PILATE
You are a king, then!

JESUS
You say that I am a king. I was born for one thing and came into the world for one thing: to witness to the truth. All who belong to the truth listen to me.

PILATE
What is truth?

Pilate's Wife Warns Him About Jesus

NARRATOR 2
While Pilate was seated for the tribunal, his wife sent him this message:

ACT TWO

PILATE'S WIFE
Under no circumstances have anything to do with that innocent man, because I have suffered tremendously today in a dream about him.

Pilate Declares
Jesus Innocent

NARRATOR 1
With this he went out again to the chief priests, the rulers along with the crowd of people, and said to them,

PILATE
You brought me this man as one who was corrupting people and I have examined him in your presence. I have found nothing with respect to your charges against him. Neither did Herod, because he sent him back to us. Surely you can see he has done nothing to deserve death. I will punish him, therefore, and then release him.

THE LAST DAY

Release of Barabbas

NARRATOR 2

Now at the festival it was the governor's custom to release a prisoner chosen by the crowd. At that time they were holding a well-known prisoner named Barabbas. Pilate said to them,

PILATE

You have a custom that I release for you one prisoner at the time of Passover. Do you want me to release 'the king of the Jews'? Do you want me to release Jesus Barabbas, or do you want me to release Jesus who is called the Messiah?

NARRATOR 1

Because he knew it was out of envy that they had delivered Jesus to him. They shouted back,

CROWD

No! Give us Barabbas!

ACT TWO

NARRATOR 2

Now Barabbas was a robber. But the chief priests and the elders persuaded the crowd to ask for Barabbas and to have Jesus put to death.

Pilate asked,

PILATE

Then what will I do with Jesus who is called Christ?

NARRATOR 1

They all answered,

CROWD

Crucify him!

PILATE

For what? What evil has he done?

NARRATOR 2

But the crowd shouted all the more,

CROWD

Crucify! Crucify him!

The Last Day

NARRATOR 1
Pilate saw that he wasn't getting anywhere, but that instead a riot was beginning. He took water and washed his hands in front of the crowd and said,

PILATE
I am innocent of this man's blood. See how this is your doing!

NARRATOR 2
The whole crowd answered,

CROWD
His blood be upon us and upon our children!

NARRATOR 1
Then Pilate released Barabbas.

ACT TWO

Jesus Is Scourged And Crowned With Thorns

NARRATOR 2

So Pilate took Jesus and had him lashed with a whip. The guards then led Jesus into an interior courtyard of the *Praetorium* and called together the entire troop of soldiers. They stripped his clothes off of him and placed a purple robe around his shoulders. They braided a crown of thorns and placed it on his head and put a staff in his right hand. Falling on their knees, they began to mock-praise him with,

SOLDIERS

Hail, king of the Jews!

NARRATOR 1

They spit on him, and took the staff and beat him on the head. They slapped him.

The Last Day

*Jesus Is
Presented Again
To The Crowd*

NARRATOR 2
Pilate came out again and said to the crowd,

PILATE
Listen! I am bringing him outside to you so that you will know that I found no substantial charges against him.

NARRATOR 1
Jesus came outside wearing the thorn crown and the purple robe, and Pilate said,

PILATE
Here is the man!

NARRATOR 2
When the chief priests and their attendants saw him, they shouted,

PRIESTS AND ATTENDANTS
Crucify! Crucify!

ACT TWO

PILATE
Take him and crucify him yourselves. But as for me, I have found no substantial charge against him.

NARRATOR 1
But the Judeans insisted,

ONE OF THE CHIEF PRIESTS
We have a law, and according to that law he deserves death, because he claimed he was the Son of God.

NARRATOR 2
So when Pilate heard these words, he grew even more afraid. He went inside the *Praetorium* again and asked Jesus,

PILATE
Where do you come from?

NARRATOR 1
But Jesus didn't give him an answer.

PILATE
Do you refuse to speak even to me? Do you not understand? I have authority to set you free and I have authority to crucify you.

The Last Day

JESUS
You would not have power over me at all if it were not given to you from above. So the one who handed me over to you has greater sin than you.

NARRATOR 2
At this Pilate searched for a way to set Jesus free, but the Judeans called out,

ONE OF THE CHIEF PRIESTS
If you release this man you are not a friend of Caesar. Anyone who makes himself out to be a king speaks against Caesar.

NARRATOR 1
So then, when Pilate heard these words, he brought Jesus out and sat down in the tribunal seat at the place known as the Stone Pavement but in Aramaic is called *Gabbatha.*

NARRATOR 2
Now it was about the sixth hour on the day of preparation for the Passover.

ACT TWO

PILATE
Here is your king!

CROWD
Take him! Take him! Crucify him!

PILATE
Your king? Crucify your king?

ONE OF THE CHIEF PRIESTS
We have no king but Caesar.

NARRATOR 1
So Pilate handed Jesus over to be crucified.

NARRATOR 2
So the soldiers took Jesus. After they had mocked him, they stripped off the purple robe and put his own clothes back on him.

THE LAST DAY

From The Praetorium To Golgotha

Jesus Carries The Cross

SETTING: The streets of Jerusalem leading from the *Praetorium*, out the city gate, and to the place of execution

NARRATOR 1
Carrying the cross himself, he went out toward the place of the Skull, which is called Golgotha in Aramaic.

Simon Of Cyrene Is Compelled To Carry The Cross

NARRATOR 2
As they went out of the city gate they met a man from Cyrene, named Simon, who was passing by on his way in from the country. Simon was the father of Alexander and Rufus. They put the cross on him and forced him to carry it behind Jesus.

ACT TWO

*Jesus Speaks To
Those Who Are
Following Him*

NARRATOR 1
Now following him there was a large number of people, including women who loudly mourned and wailed for him. But Jesus turned and said to them,

JESUS
Daughters of Jerusalem, do not weep for me, but weep for yourselves and for your children, because certainly the days are coming when it will be said,

'Childless women are the ones who are blessed;

the wombs that did not give birth

and the breasts that never nursed!'

Then

" 'they will begin to say to the mountains, "Fall on us!"

and to the hills, "Cover us!"'

Because if they do these things when the sap is in the tree, what will happen when it is dry?

THE LAST DAY

Jesus Arrives At The Place of Execution

NARRATOR 2
Two others, who were criminals, were being led to be crucified with him.

They brought Jesus to the place called Golgotha, which means "The Place of the Skull."

SETTING: A place outside of the city gates that was used for executions

Jesus Is Offered Wine To Drink

NARRATOR 1
They offered Jesus wine to drink, mixed with something bitter. And he tasted it but he did not drink it.

ACT TWO

Jesus Is Crucified

NARRATOR 2
There they crucified him.

SOUND OF NAIL BEING HAMMERED INTO WOOD.

PAUSE

Jesus Is Stripped And The Soldiers Divide His Clothing

JESUS
Father, forgive them, for they don't know what they are doing.

NARRATOR 1
When they had nailed him to the cross they took his clothes and divided them into four shares, one for each of them, with the tunic held out. They distributed his clothes among themselves by chance, casting lots to determine what each one would get. The tunic was woven in one piece from top to bottom, without seams.

The Last Day

SOLDIER

Let's not tear it. Let's cast a lot for whose it will be.

NARRATOR 2

This happened in order to fulfill the scripture:

"They divided my garments among them

and cast lots for my clothing."

NARRATOR 1

Then they sat down and they kept watch over him. It was the third hour when they crucified him.

A Written Sign
Of The
Charges Is
Placed Over His
Head

NARRATOR 2

Pilate had a notice prepared and fastened to the cross above his head with the written charge against him. And the notice of the charge read: Jesus of Nazareth, the king of the Judeans.

ACT TWO

NARRATOR 1
Many Judeans read this sign because the place where Jesus was crucified was near the city, and it was written in Aramaic, Latin and Greek. That led to a protest by the Judean chief priests. They said to Pilate,

SETTING: The *Praetorium*; the residential palace of the Roman governor, Pontius Pilate

ONE OF THE CHIEF PRIESTS
Do not write 'The King of the Jews.' But instead write that this man claimed to be king of the Jews.

PILATE
What I have written is written.

The Last Day

*Jesus Speaks To
His Mother
And To The
Beloved Disciple*

SETTING: A place outside of the city gates that was used for executions

NARRATOR 2

Near the cross of Jesus stood his mother, his mother's sister, Mary the wife of Clopas, and Mary Magdalene. So when Jesus saw his mother standing nearby and one disciple whom he loved next to her, he said to his mother,

JESUS
Woman, here is your son.

NARRATOR 1
Then to the disciple,

JESUS
Here is your mother.

ACT TWO

NARRATOR 2
From that very hour this disciple took her into his home.

*Jesus Speaks
To The Two
Criminals*

NARRATOR 1
And with him they crucified two robbers, one on his right and one on his left, with Jesus in between.

Then one of the criminals hanging there jeered at him:

FIRST CRIMINAL
You're the Messiah, aren't you? Save yourself and us!

NARRATOR 2
But the other criminal answered him with a reprimand.

The Last Day

SECOND CRIMINAL
Don't you fear God, since you received the same sentence? It is right for us to be punished, because we are getting back what our actions deserve. But this man did nothing wrong.

PAUSE

SECOND CRIMINAL
(continuing)
Jesus, remember me when you come into your kingdom.

JESUS
I promise you, today you will be with me in paradise.

Insults To Jesus

NARRATOR 1
And also some who passed by jeered at him, shaking their heads they said,

FIRST PASSERBY
This one who was going to destroy the temple and in three days build it! Save yourself! If you really are the Son of God, come down from the cross!

ACT TWO

NARRATOR 2
And likewise the chief priests, the teachers of the law and the elders were ridiculing him. They said,

ONE OF THE CHIEF PRIESTS
Sarcastically

He saved others, but he isn't able to save himself! Some king of Israel he is! Now would be a good time for us to see this "Christ," this "King of Israel," come down from the cross, if we are supposed to believe.

'He trusts in God. Let God rescue him now if he wills it.'

Didn't he say, 'I am the Son of God?'

NARRATOR 1
And the chief priests and scribes ridiculed him to one another,

SCRIBE
"He saved others, but he can't save himself!"

The Last Day

NARRATOR 2
The soldiers also approached him and ridiculed him. They offered him bitter wine and they said,

SOLDIER
If you are the king of Judea save yourself!

Darkness Covers The Land

NARRATOR 1
Darkness came over the whole land at around noon, until three in the afternoon, because the sun's light deserted the land.

Jesus Cries Out To God

NARRATOR 2
Then at about three in the afternoon, Jesus cried out in a loud voice,

JESUS
Eloi, Eloi, l'ma sabachthani?

ACT TWO

NARRATOR 1
That means, "My God, my God, why have you forsaken me?"

Upon hearing this, some of those standing nearby said,

FIRST PASSERBY
Listen, this man is calling Elijah.

*Jesus Is Offered
A Sponge Full
of Bitter Wine*

NARRATOR 2
Someone ran and got a sponge. He filled it with bitter wine, put it on a pole, and offered it to Jesus to drink. But the rest said,

SECOND PASSERBY
Wait. Leave him alone. Let's see if Elijah comes to save him.

NARRATOR 1
After this, Jesus, when he knew that everything had now been completed, in order to fulfill the Scripture, said,

JESUS
I thirst.

The Last Day

NARRATOR 2
A container full of bitter wine lay there, so they took a soaked sponge of the bitter wine wrapped around a bunch hyssop stalks, and brought it to his mouth.

The Last Breath Of Jesus

NARRATOR 1
When he had taken the bitter wine, Jesus said,

JESUS
It is completed.

with a loud voice

Father, into your hands I entrust my spirit.

NARRATOR 2
With that, he bowed his head and gave up his spirit and he breathed his last.

ACT TWO

*After Jesus
Dies The
Curtain is Torn
Open*

NARRATOR 1

And look! The curtain of the temple was torn in two from top to bottom. The earth quaked, the rocks split, and the tombs were opened. Many bodies of saints who slept were awakened and they came out of the tombs after the resurrection of Jesus and went into the holy city and showed themselves to many people.

*Reaction To
The Death of
Jesus*

NARRATOR 2

When the centurion guarding Jesus and those who were with him saw the earthquake and all the things that had happened, and saw how he died, they were terrified. The centurion praised God, then said,

The Last Day

CENTURION
Surely this man was innocent. In truth, he was the Son of God!

NARRATOR 1
When the entire crowd who had gathered to see all of this experienced the unfolding of these events, they pounded their chests and went away.

The Women Who Followed Jesus Were Looking On

NARRATOR 2
But all those who knew him, including the women who had followed Jesus from Galilee serving him, stood at a distance watching what happened. Among them were Mary Magdalene, Mary the mother of James the younger and Joseph, the mother of Zebedee's sons, and Salome. Many other women who had come up to Jerusalem with him were also there.

ACT TWO

*The Side of
Jesus is Pierced*

NARRATOR 1

Now the Judean leaders did not want the bodies left on the crosses during the Sabbath. Since it was the day of Preparation for the next day, especially because this was to be a special Sabbath, they asked Pilate to have the legs of the crucified men broken and their bodies taken down.

NARRATOR 2

So the soldiers came and broke the legs of the first one, and then those of the other who had been crucified with Jesus. But they found Jesus already dead when they came to him so they did not break his legs, but one of the soldiers pierced his side with a spear and a flow of blood and water came out right away.

The Last Day

NARRATOR 1

The one who saw these things has given witness, and his testimony is true. And concerning these things he knows that he speaks the truth, so you too may believe. For this happened in order that the scripture would be fulfilled. "His bones will not be broken," and, as another scripture says, "They will look on the one they pierced."

Jesus Is Taken Down From The Cross

SETTING: The *Praetorium*; the residential palace of the Roman governor, Pontius Pilate

NARRATOR 2

As evening approached, there came a rich man from Arimathea, named Joseph. He went boldly to Pilate and made a request for permission to remove body of Jesus. Joseph was a disciple of Jesus, but secretly because he was afraid of the Judean leaders.

ACT TWO

NARRATOR1

Joseph was a member of the Council of some stature, who was waiting with hope for the kingdom of God. He was a good and just man, who had not given his consent to the determination or action of the Council.

NARRATOR 2

Pilate wondered if Jesus was already dead. He called the centurion and questioned him as to whether Jesus had already died. And when he learned from the centurion that Jesus was dead, Pilate gave the order for the body to be released to Joseph.

SETTING: A place of execution outside the city walls

NARRATOR 1

So he came and removed the body. And Nicodemus came also, the one who had first visited Jesus at night. He brought a mixture of myrrh and aloes weighing around seventy-five pounds.

THE LAST DAY

*The Body Of
Jesus Is
Prepared For
Burial*

NARRATOR 2

Joseph took the body, and the two of them wrapped it in a clean linen cloth with the aromatic spices in the ordinary way the Judeans prepare for burial.

*Jesus Is Laid In
A Tomb And
A Stone Is
Rolled Across
The Entrance*

SETTING: A garden near the place of execution that was used for burials

NARRATOR 1

Now there was a garden at the place where Jesus was crucified. And in the garden was a new tomb, in which no body had ever been laid. Since the tomb was nearby, and because it was the Jewish day of Preparation, Joseph placed Jesus in his own new tomb that he had cut out of the rock.

ACT TWO

NARRATOR 2

Now the women who followed Jesus from Galilee came along following Joseph. They saw the tomb and how his body was placed into it. Joseph rolled a great stone in front of the door to the tomb and went away.

NARRATOR 1

Mary Magdalene and Mary the mother of Joseph were sitting there opposite the tomb and saw where his body was laid. Then they returned to where they were staying and prepared aromatic spices and myrrh. And they observed the Sabbath by resting, obeying the commandment.

END OF ACT II

Acknowledgments

I am grateful to Chapel by the Lake in Juneau, Alaska, for hosting the premier of *The Last Day* as a Readers Theater performance. Special thanks to Emily Fergusson for her masterful work directing the premier.

The *Down The Last Road* series

What started as a single blended translation has grown into four publications designed to make the story easy to use for individuals, for families, and for churches. This series of resources has been developed in order to present this story in the best possible ways for different audiences. Consider how you might use these to present this narrative in ways that will serve various needs. Whether sitting quietly alone, simply reading the simple story, or encountering narrative in other creative ways, you can make this day in the life of Jesus a life-changing part of how you see the world. Four different publications are available make the meaning of this story more vivid in your experience.

Down The Last Road
The Last Day of the Earthly Life of Jesus

This blended narrative presents a complete account of everything the Gospels report concerning the last day of the earthly life of Jesus. Included in this volume you will find a simple, meditational version of the narrative, along with *Study Notes* with all of the scripture references included in detail.

This book presents the basic form of the narrative that is used for each of these resources.

The Last Day

A Play In Two Acts

This script contains the complete narrative of that last day, from just before the last supper up to the moment when the remaining friends of Jesus walked away from his tomb. The script was created straight from the text of the blended translation. All quotations were simply converted into spoken parts for the characters in the play. A narrator's part utilizes the precise words from the Gospels to set the scene for the dialogue that takes place.

The play is designed to be presented as a Readers Theater performance, so no costumes, sets, or line memorization is required.

Separated into 2 Acts, the play may either be presented all at once, or in two separate performances. Act 1 covers the events of Maundy Thursday, from the Upper Room to the arrest in the garden. Act 2 moves to the trial, abuse, and crucifixion. With a little planning you will be able to perform either a 2 Act play on Maundy Thursday, or put on or 2 separate performances on Maundy Thursday and Good Friday.

For the sake of facilitating performance, the script is available in two forms.

THE LAST DAY

DIRECTOR'S SCRIPT

With extensive instructions, suggestions and notes, the Director's version of the script covers everything a director will want to know to lead a group of readers to perform the play. This will guide your preparations and help you know how many copies of the READER'S SCRIPT will be needed.

THE LAST DAY

READER'S SCRIPT

This contains the simple script in 2 Acts. To perform the reading, order enough copies to give one to each participant.

The number of participants may vary based on how you choose to divide the readings. Guidance for this is found in the Director's Script, and it will be helpful to read that guidance before determining the number of Reader's Scripts to order for your performance.

Scenes From The Last Journey

14 Points On The Way of the Cross

The 14 events recounted in this book come directly from the pages of the four gospels. So these are not identical with the traditional 14 stations, but rather our 14 stations have been designed to reflect the Biblical accounts from the betrayal and arrest until Jesus is laid in the tomb.

ABOUT THE AUTHOR

Richard P. Zimmerman is a pastor and writer who has served in several congregations in the Pacific Northwest and Alaska. His degrees include a BA from the University of Washington, an MDiv from Princeton Theological Seminary, a ThM from Regent College, and a DMin from Columbia Theological Seminary. He also completed a year of advanced study in Northwest Semitic Languages at the University of Chicago.

Having a special interest in the languages of the Bible world has led him to take extensive courses in Greek, Hebrew, and related languages.

Richard makes his home the Pacific Northwest with his wife, Annie. They enjoy hiking, skiing, snowboarding, golf, and just generally being outside in God's creation.

www.ingramcontent.com/pod-product-compliance
Lightning Source LLC
Chambersburg PA
CBHW072015290426
44109CB00018B/2250